'New for this issue we have .... a handful of walks which feature less mud than the rest after prolonged heavy rain.'

Welcome to the third instalment of my guides to walks in the local area. In this book you will find 21 walks all within 45 minute's drive from Stamford at the very most. These routes range from Tugby near Uppingham in the west, the Ashton Wold estate near Oundle in the south, Nene Park in the east and Corby Glen to the north. The walks feature a wide variety of waterways, woodlands, hills, flatlands, villages, churches, pubs and market towns. These are landscapes and settlements which demonstrate the area at its rural finest, and our aim is to help you enjoy every footstep.

I live in the beautiful old limestone town of Stamford and I am not ashamed to say I love it as much now as I ever have done. And it has been my pleasure to cover the local footpaths and bridleways for Active magazine for the last 10 years. With trusty labradors at my side I have scoured Ordnance Survey maps and set out in all weathers to find the most interesting routes possible. And it's an absolute pleasure to share some of my findings in this series of books. There are endless discoveries to be made from walking our area in all the seasons. Be it climbing a hill and enjoying the view, exploring a new village, strolling through ancient woodland, watching the stream gurgling by on a summer's day or just observing nature ticking along, it's a great big playground just waiting to be explored.

I am very conscious that few other countries in the world have the same public footpath system we enjoy in the UK and it seems incumbent on us to make the most of it. Particularly if there happens to be a warm and friendly public house with a suitable refreshment at the end of the route.

New for this issue we have earmarked a handful of walks which feature less mud than the rest after prolonged heavy rain. They are marked as Winter Walks (see icon left) and, while I can't promise you won't see any mud on these routes, they should be a bit better underfoot after the rain than some.

I am sure you will enjoy exploring as much as I have, but I would also urge all readers to take a navigation aid, whether that's a trusty hard copy of the OS map (still my favourite) or the OS App, it really is essential to have some extra guidance with you.

If you are undertaking one of the walks in this book please be considerate of the residents in the smaller villages and the need for emergency vehicle access when parking. Our public footpaths are there to be enjoyed, but it can be problematic in smaller villages if access is blocked.

And if you are lucky enough to be accompanied by a four-legged walking companion please clean up after them and pay attention to signs about livestock. And don't forget to close the gate.

Happy walking!

Will Hetherington

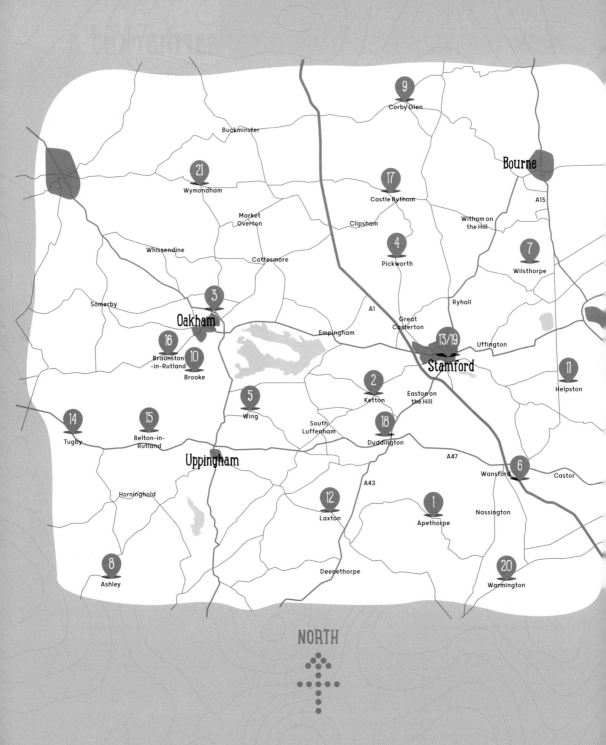

KING WEST

9 Corby Glen

Buckminster

21 Wymondham

17 Castle Bytham

Bourne

A15

Market Overton

Clipsham

Witham on the Hill

Whissendine

4 Pickworth

7 Wilsthorpe

Cottesmore

Somerby

A1

Ryhall

3 Oakham

Empingham

Great Casterton

13/19 Stamford

Uffington

16 Braunston -in-Rutland

10 Brooke

2 Ketton

Easton on the Hill

11 Helpston

5 Wing

South Luffenham

18 Duddington

14 Tugby

15 Belton-in-Rutland

A47

6 Wansford

Castor

Uppingham

A43

Horninghold

12 Laxton

1 Apethorpe

Nassington

8 Ashley

Deenethorpe

20 Warmington

NORTH

**First published in the
United Kingdom in 2022 by
Triangle Publishing Ltd
Eventus Business Centre
Sunderland Road
Market Deeping
PE6 8FD**

ISBN 978-1-8382124-2-1

This book can be ordered from the publisher at **www.theactivemag.com** or try your local bookshop.

We have taken every care to ensure these walks are up-to-date and accurate at the time of publication. If you notice any changes or errors, please let us know by email to **walks@theactivemag.com** We will endeavour to update the information for the next printing of the book.

The maps in this guide are for illustration only and you should take your own OS map or a navigation device on all walks.

Author
Will Hetherington

Design
Matt Tarrant

Publishers
Triangle Publishing Ltd

Foreword

H ere we are again; winter is coming so it's time for another volume of Will's Walks, welcome to volume 3. Because the previous two walk books proved so popular we felt sure Will had another 21 walks in him; and he did!

It's quite incredible to think that within less than an hour from Stamford (my home town), in every direction there are so many walks to be enjoyed. Aren't we lucky to live in such a beautiful part of the countryside? And, of course, that we are able to rely on Will to offer inspiration for a short stomp or a much longer hike; thanks Will and thank you to each and every one of you who has bought a book. We have thoroughly enjoyed your enthusiasm and hearing your comments about the walks; thankfully most were very positive.

There is no doubt that getting outside in the fresh air for a brisk walk and some exercise does us good; physically and mentally and it costs nothing and warms you up – both things we might appreciate this winter. And quite often when it is the last thing you feel like doing, that little bit of effort offers the biggest reward.

I was encouraging Will to add some 'less muddy winter ones' to this volume and I'm really glad he has as now we don't necessarily need to be slip, sliding away up to our knees in mud. Less washing of dogs and boots is always a bonus as far as I'm concerned.

Enjoy the walks and remember to close the gate behind you to make sure we keep everyone happy.

Mary Bremner - Editor, Active Magazine

Active magazine, your local healthy lifestyle magazine

Inspiring people to stay healthy and enjoy a fulfilling life is the purpose behind our pages every month. We say, get off the sofa and get going!

Active is packed full of well written, interesting editorial including local features, fascinating people, health advice, local news and sport, cycle routes and, of course, walks. The magazine covers the Welland Valley including the towns of Stamford, Oakham, Uppingham, Market Harborough and Oundle, and all surrounding villages. Pick up your copy locally in supermarkets or one of our many local businesses.

Find us online at www.theactivemag.com

Facebook
theACTIVEmag

Twitter
@theACTIVEmag

Instagram
theactivemaguk

Contents

UP TO FOUR MILES

1. APETHORPE
2. KETTON QUARRY AND ALDGATE
3. OAKHAM CANAL
4. PICKWORTH AND THE DRIFT
5. THE CHATER VALLEY
6. WANSFORD STATION, WATER NEWTON AND SUTTON
7. WILSTHORPE AND BRACEBOROUGH

FOUR TO SIX MILES

8. ASHLEY AND STOKE ALBANY
9. CORBY GLEN, BURTON-LE-COGGLES AND SWAYFIELD
10. BROOKE, EGLETON & GUNTHORPE
11. HELPSTON
12. LAXTON HALL AND BLATHERWYCKE
13. STAMFORD AND THE WELLAND LOOP
14. TUGBY AND ROLLESTON

SIX MILES PLUS

15. BELTON-IN-RUTLAND
16. BRAUNSTON-IN-RUTLAND
17. CASTLE BYTHAM AND CLIPSHAM
18. DUDDINGTON AND KETTON
19. STAMFORD, TOLETHORPE, RYHALL AND BELMESTHORPE
20. WARMINGTON AND ASHTON WOLD
21. WYMONDHAM

ROUTE MAP KEY

 Start/finish Walk route Direction Village / Town Woodland

 Road River/lake/ reservoir Railway Church PH Public House

UP TO FOUR MILES

1. Apethorpe

**A lot of this walk is on roads and established farm tracks
so it's a good option for the wettest months of the year.**

THE ROUTE

Park responsibly somewhere near the popular Willow & Brook pub in Apethorpe and walk up the side road which heads west alongside the pub. After the tennis courts on the right you will come to a junction where you turn left following the signs to Apethorpe Grange and The Lodge. Stay on this road for three quarters of a mile with a tall line of evergreen trees on your left for much of the way. Just before you reach Cheeseman's Lodge and Lodge Farm you will see the gate on the right signposted diverted bridleway.

Go through this gate and follow the path with a small lake on your left. After the lake take the sharp left turn up towards the farm ahead and then turn right at the farm to walk west along the road. When you reach Tomlin Wood keep going across the bottom of the wood for another 500 metres and look out for the right turn in the hedgeline at the end of the wood.

Walk up the western edge of Tomlin Wood for half a mile, and look out for red kites and other birdlife as you go. At the end of the wood you will come to a road. Turn right here and walk the last mile back to Apethorpe along the tarmac access road, with some nice woodland either side and the chance to spot a deer or two along the way. When you get back to the village it's worth going for a wander before popping into the Willow & Brook for refreshment.

ESSENTIAL INFORMATION

Difficulty rating

One paw. It's fairly flat and mostly excellent underfoot with no stiles.

Where to park
Somewhere near the popular Willow & Brook pub in Apethorpe.

Distance
Three and a half miles.

Highlights
Beautiful Apethorpe, mature woodlands and mostly good underfoot even in wet weather.

The pooch perspective
It's mostly on tarmac so no livestock but also very limited fresh running water.

Apethorpe

Woodnewton

POINT OF INTEREST

Apethorpe Palace was once owned by Elizabeth I who inherited it from her father Henry VIII, and it had an important role in entertaining Tudor and Stuart monarchs. For a period it was lived in regularly by James I and Charles I.

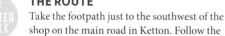

2. Ketton quarry and Aldgate

This rural/urban stroll is a lovely option at any time of the year and includes an important nature reserve managed by the Wildlife Trust.

THE ROUTE

WINTER WALK

Take the footpath just to the southwest of the shop on the main road in Ketton. Follow the path through Home Farm and then uphill for a few hundred metres and look out for the signposted right turn 100 metres after a gateway. Take this turn and follow the path around the eastern edge of a disused quarry. You will soon come to the woods and enter Ketton Quarry Site of Special Scientific Interest (SSSI), where there are rare species, such as the bee orchid and the purple hairstreak butterfly.

As long as you stay on the paths you are free to explore the SSSI, but to continue the route follow the main path through the woodland heading north. You will soon start to see industrial buildings behind the fence on your right

and you will also pass the pet cemetery on your right, which has apparently been there since the 1930s. Stay on the path and you will come out at the top of Pit Lane. Turn right here and walk downhill for nearly a kilometre, passing the guides and scouts headquarters and the sports ground along the way.

When you get to the main road at the bottom of Pit Lane, turn left and look out for the footpath to the right after 200 metres. Walk down here and, after crossing the river Chater, take the path to the right to bring you through the fields to the footbridge in Aldgate. You can turn right here and walk up Bull Lane back to the main road or carry on and explore the area around the church before you finish.

Ketton

Aldgate

PH

S/F

POINT OF INTEREST

The Leicestershire and Rutland Wildlife Trust cares for 35 nature reserves like Ketton Quarry, covering more than 3,000 acres.

ESSENTIAL INFORMATION

Difficulty rating

One paw. It's mostly excellent underfoot.

Where to park
Somewhere convenient and responsible near the main road through Ketton.

Distance
Two and a half miles.

Highlights
The wildlife in the SSSI, the disused quarry and the beautiful old houses of Aldgate and Ketton.

The pooch perspective
The dogs will enjoy the stroll but apart from a dip in the Chater there's not much in it for them.

3. Oakham canal

Thanks to a lot of hard working volunteers this area is now perfect for quiet walking and enjoying nature.

THE ROUTE

It has come as a surprise to a few people recently to discover Oakham has a canal, but a section of it is now extremely accessible for quiet walking. The old canal went from the town centre to Melton Mowbray, but the section for this walk is to the north of the bypass and runs between the railway line to the west and the road to Ashwell to the east.

A committed group of volunteers have put in plenty of hard labour resurfacing the footpaths, rebuilding steps and installing new bridges. The funds came from a registered charity and it's wonderful to see the regeneration of what was a tired area, almost completely unfit for walking.

There are a number of access points into the walking area, and you can just start from the centre of Oakham, but that does involve a labyrinthine route through the housing estates. So I parked in the good-sized layby just east of the railway crossing on Burley Road between Langham and the Enterprise Park, which gives access to the canal halfway along the renovated section. You can also park in the layby next to Kimball Close at the northern end of the canal (or potentially even in the Enterprise Park).

Thanks to the new permissive path along the western side of the canal it's now possible to do a very pleasant loop of this wildlife haven, which is also used by the Oakham Angling Society. From the layby by the railway crossing take the permissive path north through the woods along the west side of the canal to the layby at Kimball Close. Loop round the top end of the canal and then take the path south along the eastern side. Cross Burley Road at the halfway point, and after about half a mile there is a wooden bridge on the right, which leads back to the western side and into the woods. Alternatively you can walk on from here into the fields north of the bypass.

The team, led by Paul Dadford, have done a tremendous job with the walkway and there is abundant birdlife down in this peaceful oasis. It's worth a visit any time.

ESSENTIAL INFORMATION

Difficulty rating

It's a flat path next to a canal.

Where to park
In the layby just to the east of the railway crossing on Burley Road, in the layby next to Kimball Close at the northern end, or in the Enterprise Park.

Distance
The shortest loop is just over one mile but if you venture further south to Oakham it can be longer if you wish. Or if you start in Oakham and walk out, doing the full loop, it's about four miles.

Highlights
Lovely new footpaths, birdlife and a sense of calm.

The pooch perspective
Dogs are not allowed in the canal and it's pretty limited for them.

Oakham

POINT OF INTEREST
Paul Dadford is a local man who first started to think about improving the pathways around the canal eight years ago and the charity has now been running for two years: oakhamcanal.org

4. Pickworth and the Drift

Most of this route is on excellent farm tracks and tarmac so it's a good winter option.

THE ROUTE

The Drift heads east away from Pickworth at the main junction in the village. Walk gradually uphill along this ancient drover's track and you will soon be transported to one of the most peaceful places in the whole area. Stay on the track for more than a mile, passing Turnpole Wood on the right as you go, and you will eventually come to a smart red brick house on the left, with a few other houses behind it. Here you will find the gate in the hedge on the right taking you off the Drift and into the farmland beyond the hedge.

The path heads south west for a few hundred yards before coming to a small plantation. Follow the sign into the plantation and take the right turn within 100 yards. Then you will very soon come to the main farm track. Turn right here and after another 200 yards turn left at the sign. Stay on the track following the footpath signs for another kilometre and, if you are lucky, you may see a few hares out on the fields to the left and right. When you reach the no entry sign on the farm track take the right turn off the track and on to the grassy path along the northern edge of a piece of woodland.

It's a nice change of scene for a few hundred yards before you reach Pickworth Road ahead. Turn right and walk the last three quarters of a mile along the road, passing Taylor's Farm and Christian's Lodge along the way. This is not a busy stretch of road and helps make this walk a good choice in the wettest and muddiest months of the year.

ESSENTIAL INFORMATION

Difficulty rating

One paw. It's fairly flat and mostly on farm tracks and roads. No stiles.

Where to park
Responsibly in Pickworth.

Distance
Four miles.

Highlights
An extremely quiet and peaceful piece of countryside and pretty little Pickworth. Brown hares if you are lucky.

The pooch perspective
This is mostly arable land so very little livestock, although there isn't really any fresh water on the route either.

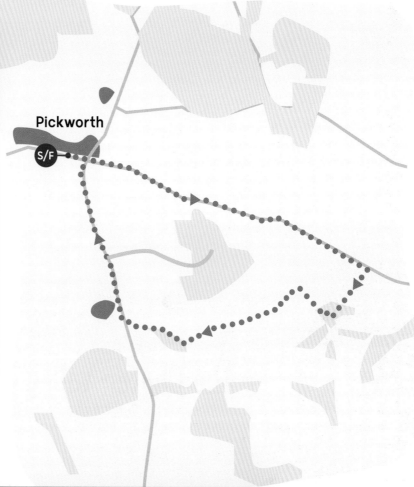

POINT OF INTEREST

John Clare, the nationally acclaimed 'Peasant Poet', spent his early working life in Pickworth as a labourer in the limekiln in the early 1800s and met his future wife on Walk Farm which features heavily in this route.

5. The Chater valley

Three villages in the heart of Rutland and some blissfully quiet countryside make for the perfect Sunday stroll.

THE ROUTE

Park on Morcott Road on the eastern edge of Wing and walk east out of the village. Just after you pass the last houses on the left you will see a lane running downhill to the left. Don't walk down the lane but you will see a footpath sign in the trees just after the lane on the left. Take this path and follow it through two small fields, past a farm on the left and then across another larger field. You will then cross the minor road that runs down to Lyndon and keep heading east across the next bigger field. If the path is not clearly visible (it wasn't when I last walked this way) then aim just left of the woodland ahead.

You will find the next stage starting in a gap in the hedge to the north of the wood. From here there is a path with a tall hedge on the left and a fence on the right, which leads to Pinfold Lane on the edge of Pilton. It's worth a very short stroll into Pilton, one of Rutland's very quietest settlements, but to continue the walk turn left on Pinfold Lane and head downhill along the road.

You will soon pass the signposted entrance to Chater Valley Farm on the left and then go underneath the railway before reaching the junction. Turn right here, cross the bridge and continue uphill along the magnificent tree-lined avenue towards Lyndon. Just as you reach Lyndon take the path on the left and pass one stunning red brick house and then Lyndon Hall itself. Perhaps you can allow yourself a few delusions of grandeur as you do so.

Follow the path into a narrow band of woodland and then turn sharp left, followed by a right turn along the next hedgerow. Another left turn at the end of this field will put you on the farm track which winds down to the bridge over the Chater, a good spot for the dogs to have a dip and a drink. Cross the bridge and now you have a choice. You can keep going straight uphill (over the railway) on the farm track, which will bring you out on the eastern edge of Wing. Or you can turn right immediately after the bridge and then left in 100 metres and follow the path over the railway and then up into Wing where Church Street meets Bottom Street. This second option is more scenic but there are often cattle in the last field before you get into the village.

POINT OF INTEREST

Just off Glaston Road in Wing there is a turf cut maze, one of just eight remaining in England. Technically it's a labyrinth, 14 metres in diameter, with one grass path that winds and backtracks before leading to the centre. There are many theories about the origins of these turf mazes, including references to the classical Cretan labyrinth.

Lyndon

Wing

PH

S/F

ESSENTIAL INFORMATION

Difficulty rating

Two paws. Half the walk is on farm tracks and country lanes and the rest is not challenging.

Where to park
On Morcott Road (the main street) in Wing.

Distance
Three and a half miles.

Highlights
The peace and quiet of the Chater Valley, the tree-lined avenue into Wing and the grandeur of Lyndon Hall.

The pooch perspective
The Chater comes in handy at the right time. There can be cattle in the field below Bottom Street in Wing at the end of the walk, but you can take the farm track back into the village (after the bridge over the Chater) if that's a problem.

6. Wansford Station, Water Newton and Sutton

A tremendous walk with plenty of interest in the Nene Park Rural Estate.

THE ROUTE

The first thing you need to know is that Wansford Station is not in Wansford. It's a mile south east and off a different junction on the A1. You will know you are in the right place when you find the Nene Valley Railway headquarters, where there is ample parking along the roadside.

To start the walk cross the Nene on the footbridge adjacent to the railway bridge and turn right at the bottom of the steps, following the sign for River Route - Nene Way, and keeping the river on your immediate right. In half a mile turn right on to the footbridge across the weir (the river splits into two here) and keep going with the southern branch of the river still on your right. You will soon walk through a thin belt of trees and see the beautiful setting of Water Newton on the opposite bank.

Walk until you get to the lock and then turn left and follow the path north east and you will soon cross the northern branch of the river on a wide bridge. Keep heading north east over the railway track (there is a useful map of the Nene Park Rural Estate just before the railway) and then on to Station Road.

You will pass the Station Master's garden on your left and then stay on the tarmac for about 500 metres until you pass a bench and a bin next to a gate and a lane on your right. At the next gateway on the left turn left on to the bridleway. Unhelpfully there is no signpost here but the route is clearly marked on the map by the railway. Stay on the farm track for a quarter of a mile until you get to the course of Ermine Street, the old Roman Road, and turn right here (again there is no signpost but it's pretty obvious). These days it's a very pleasant grassy track which leads to the site of the Sutton Cross, where there is a plaque explaining this was a Saxon meeting place.

The path also meets the road here but turn left immediately to take the footpath into the eastern edge of sleepy little Sutton. Stay on the road into the village, passing Sutton Lodge as you do, and after the bridge over the dismantled railway turn left on to Lovers Lane just before the church. At the bottom of the lane turn right at the signpost to Wansford Station circular route and follow the signs over the wetlands back to the car.

ESSENTIAL INFORMATION

Difficulty rating

Two paws. It's pretty flat around here but it is four miles.

Where to park
At Wansford Station - please note not Wansford village.

Distance
Four miles.

Highlights
The serenity of the mill, lock and church at Water Newton and sleepy little Sutton. The sweeping river Nene, a Roman road, a Saxon meeting place and a steam railway. There's even a Lovers Lane!

The pooch perspective
There may be some grazing livestock but there's a great swimming area in the northern branch of the Nene just south of the railway.

POINT OF INTEREST

Sutton Cross was a Saxon wayside cross and was the meeting place of the council of the Nassaburgh Hundred. It was sited at the junction of Ermine Street and two important local roads and there was a Roman fort in the field opposite.

Ailsworth

Sutton

Stibbington

Castor

PH

Wansford Station

S/F

Water Newton

7. Wilsthorpe and Braceborough

Relax in the tranquility provided by this rural backwater,
and enjoy a skyline dominated by an impressive church spire.

THE ROUTE

I parked on the road right by the church in Wilsthorpe. The public footpath heads south west out of Wilsthorpe across the road from the church, and this stretch is also part of the Macmillan Way. Initially you walk down a wide gravel drive then over a couple of grass fields before reaching the arable land beyond with the Manor House over to your left. Go under the power lines and you will soon come to the metal bridge over the East Glen river. There are times of the year when there is minimal flow in this waterway, and the bridge crosses the river just 400 metres west of the point where it joins forces with the West Glen River.

Cross the bridge and keep heading south across a big field for another 200 metres, then go through the hedgerow and turn right. Stay on the path as it goes around a small spinney and then after 100 yards or so turn right and cross over the new wooden bridge through the gap in the hedge. (If you have the time and the inclination you can make a short detour to Greatford at this point and then retrace your steps).

From here head north across one big arable field and then one smaller ridge and furrow type wild meadow with two or three lovely trees in the field edges.

You will arrive in Braceborough on the village green and see the church and Braceborough Hall Nursing Home straight ahead. It's worth a stroll around the peaceful little place but to follow the route you need to turn right as soon as you get into the village. Follow the path through a farmyard then out on to the fields on a well established road. From the edge of the village it's less than one kilometre back to the metal bridge over the East Glen and Wilsthorpe beyond.

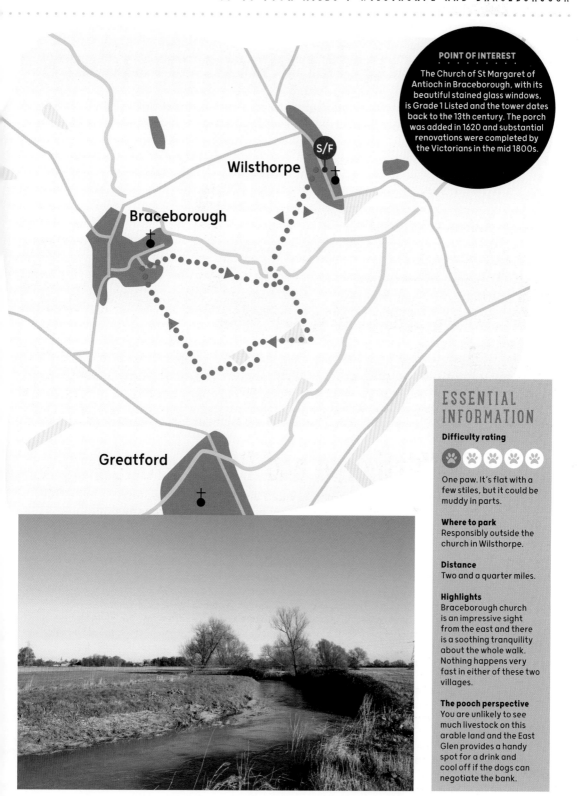

POINT OF INTEREST

The Church of St Margaret of Antioch in Braceborough, with its beautiful stained glass windows, is Grade 1 Listed and the tower dates back to the 13th century. The porch was added in 1620 and substantial renovations were completed by the Victorians in the mid 1800s.

S/F

Wilsthorpe

Braceborough

Greatford

ESSENTIAL INFORMATION

Difficulty rating

One paw. It's flat with a few stiles, but it could be muddy in parts.

Where to park
Responsibly outside the church in Wilsthorpe.

Distance
Two and a quarter miles.

Highlights
Braceborough church is an impressive sight from the east and there is a soothing tranquility about the whole walk. Nothing happens very fast in either of these two villages.

The pooch perspective
You are unlikely to see much livestock on this arable land and the East Glen provides a handy spot for a drink and cool off if the dogs can negotiate the bank.

Your countryside insiders

At **King West**, we love where you live. Our knowledge of the East Midlands countryside is what sets us apart. We sell beautiful homes in areas we would choose to live in ourselves.

There is nothing quite like country living, but you need to know where to go to have the best experience. Whether it's the ideal countryside walk with a muddy dog, where to connect with the area's heritage, or what to do with the whole family on the weekend – at King West we live and breathe the rural lifestyle. Read on for some of our team's top picks from this lovely, unspoilt region.

Stephen King
Director
Leicestershire

With our office in the heart of Market Harborough, we are truly spoilt with the variety of independent shops and eateries that surround us. Architectural gems abound in this historic market town; my favourite is The Old Grammar School nestled in Church Square.

The Welland Valley boasts rolling hills and scenery best enjoyed on foot, with circular walks from most of the local villages. The Langton Caudle walk starts near the Baker's Arms in Thorpe Langton and winds up from the village, giving spectacular views.

Tom Wilson
Director
Rutland

Though Rutland is small, it is mighty! There is much to explore in this beautiful county. Rutland Water offers countless activities and whilst the children might prefer the summertime Aqua Park, I'd rather visit the nature reserve to see the ospreys (a good excuse for a pit stop at The Horse & Jockey Inn at Manton). Oakham and Uppingham are steeped in history with stunning architecture to gaze at, which makes weekly shopping trips a bit more interesting - not many towns can boast a castle!

Ben Ainscough
Director
Nottinghamshire

As a land agent, I am obsessive about the countryside both in and out of work. I love taking my children to explore Clumber Park and Sherwood Forest, the legendary stomping ground of Robin Hood. Welbeck Abbey, Thoresby Hall, Clumber House and Workshop Manor are all famous stately homes housed in the Dukeries region and steeped in history.

Lois Simpson
Associate
Lincolnshire

Having lived in Lincolnshire for most of my life, I could wax lyrical about the wonders of this county: the golden beaches and North Sea Observatory at Chapel Point; the undulating beauty of The Wolds, which can be easily accessed from the quaint market town of Louth; to the enchanting, ancient city of Lincoln with its infamous Steep Hill. Stamford, where I now call home, means bustling Georgian streets bursting with amazing independent businesses. At weekends I meander in the grounds of the iconic Burghley House, a joy I try not to take for granted.

Helen Greaves
Business Manager
Derbyshire

Carsington Water in the Derbyshire Dales is perfect for a lakeside stroll, preferably with a stop at the hamlet of Hopton to admire Hopton Hall and its pretty gardens. Nearby, Dovedale is always worth a visit – it's best out of season when there are fewer tourists! Of course, no trip to Derbyshire is complete without a visit to the ever-beautiful Chatsworth House for stunning scenery throughout the year – daffodils in spring, rhododendrons in summer, to the changing canopies of autumn. The rolling parkland and picture-perfect estate villages are reminiscent of Downton Abbey (but without the drama).

Rural experts at your service

King West's experienced, professional property and land team specialise in rural residential sales and estate management. You couldn't be in safer hands than with one of our dedicated team. We understand that our clients are caretakers of our special countryside and properties, so we work closely with landowners and homeowners to ensure the longevity and profitability of these precious assets. We believe that our region should be loved and enjoyed by many generations to come.

10 Church Square, Market Harborough, Leicestershire, LE16 7NB
Tel: **01858 435970**

13 St Mary's Street, Stamford, Lincolnshire, PE9 2DE
Tel: **01780 484520**

kingwest.co.uk

FOUR TO SIX MILES

8. Ashley and Stoke Albany

If you don't mind a bit of mud and a couple of hills then this walk will deliver rich rewards.

THE ROUTE

Park in Ashley and take the footpath which heads west away from the village where Main Street joins Stoke Albany Road. If it's been quite wet recently there is a good chance of mud in the early stages, but just plough on and think of the workout your legs are getting. The path goes almost straight and gradually uphill through three fields (some with livestock on the day I walked here) for about half a mile before you turn left along a field boundary. Follow this and continue to gain height until you ultimately come to the wonderful six-way junction at the top of the hill. This is an unusual signpost in this wild spot and there can't be too many like it in the UK. Make sure you take the second of two options to Stoke Albany, which will have you walking on a slight diagonal towards the middle of the hedgerow on the southern edge of the field.

When you reach the field boundary you will have a tremendous view to the south taking in Stoke Albany Golf Club and the hills of Dingley and Brampton Ash. There is a small private grave fenced off to the left but your route lies directly ahead and downhill past the solitary tree. After five minutes at the most you will see the path quite obviously veering off to the left. Follow this and it will take you through a small wood with low hanging branches, and then through some big fields with the golf course to your right over the hedge. You will ultimately come to the

access road to the golf course near the clubhouse, but it's clear where the path continues over the road. Continue through (or around if necessary) the next field and you will come out on to the road just to the north of Stoke Albany. Walk into the village and then turn left and out past the very pretty St Botolph church. From here head north paying close attention to any signs there are and your OS map to ensure you keep to the path as it meanders over a couple of streams and around some woodland. I had to stop and work out exactly how to follow the path when it started going uphill because I couldn't see any signage, so do make sure you have a map or the OS App.

Once you are sure you are on the right track just to the east of Lower Lodge Farm you will see the path clearly stretching ahead so keep heading north over two hills until you see Ashley spread out in the valley before you. The views ahead and behind on this stretch are really special and sometimes it seems like you are in a much more remote part of the country than Northamptonshire.

Unfortunately at the bottom of this last hill the path goes through just about the muckiest gateway I have encountered in this area to get you back into Ashley. It's where the cows also enter the field from the neighbouring yard, which explains the problem. If you have your map you may be able to circumnavigate this gateway to the west, which I would advise. And then you are back in the village.

ESSENTIAL INFORMATION

Difficulty rating

Four paws. With the hills and the mud this is far from an easy option.

Where to park
The main road in Ashley.

Distance
Five miles.

Highlights
The beautiful views from the hilltops, Stoke Albany church, the village of Ashley and the six-way footpath junction at the top of the hill.

The pooch perspective
There is some livestock on the way round so take care. There are a couple of streams on the return leg from Stoke Albany to Ashley and one down by the golf course.

POINT OF INTEREST

Rich local ironstone was used in the extensive re-building of Ashley in the Victorian era and this enhances the beauty of the settlement, particularly around the Grade 1 listed church of St Mary the Virgin in the heart of the village

S/F
PH
Ashley

Wilbarston

Dingley

Stoke Albany
PH

Brampton Ash

9. Corby Glen, Burton-le-Coggles and Swayfield

Rolling hills, plenty of pubs and the East Coast mainline are dominant features of this walk.

THE ROUTE

Park wherever you can in Corby Glen and walk north along the High Street until you get to Tanner's Lane on the left. Turn left here and look out for the footpath sign on the right after about 150 metres. Take this path and you will soon be in open country. Follow the path and cross the West Glen river. When you get to the B1176 turn right and walk along the road before turning left to Burton-le-Coggles in a couple of minutes. Follow the road into the village and turn left on to Post Office Lane. Just after you go under the East Coast mainline turn left. This pretty much straight path goes through a few undulations and field boundaries and crosses the A151 before reaching the southern edge of Swayfield in a mile and a half.

After you cross the little wooden bridge just before the last hill up to Swayfield look out for the left turn in 100 metres (unless you want to explore the village). Follow

the path north east and go under the East Coast mainline again. Cross the road shortly afterwards and then head downhill over quite a muddy field to the West Glen river. Cross the bridge and turn left through the woodland until you come to another stile. Turn right here and walk up the hill and then back into Corby Glen to explore the village and seek refreshment.

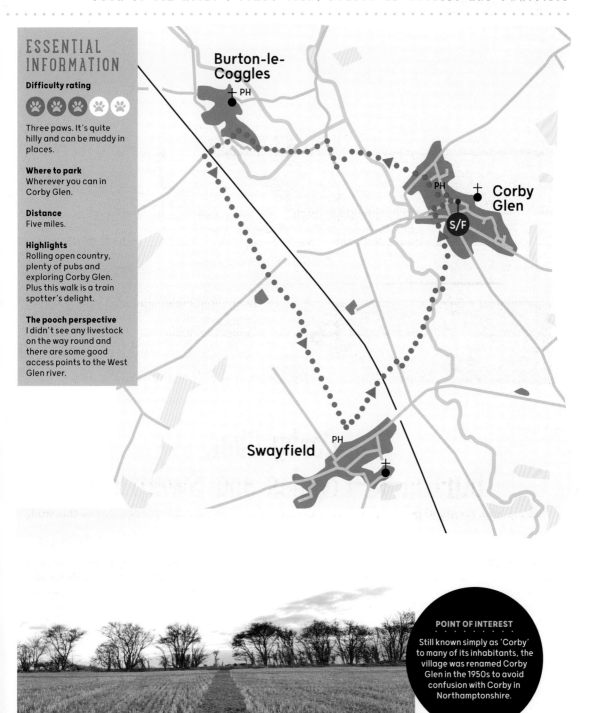

ESSENTIAL INFORMATION

Difficulty rating

Three paws. It's quite hilly and can be muddy in places.

Where to park
Wherever you can in Corby Glen.

Distance
Five miles.

Highlights
Rolling open country, plenty of pubs and exploring Corby Glen. Plus this walk is a train spotter's delight.

The pooch perspective
I didn't see any livestock on the way round and there are some good access points to the West Glen river.

Burton-le-Coggles

PH

Corby Glen

PH

S/F

Swayfield

PH

POINT OF INTEREST

Still known simply as 'Corby' to many of its inhabitants, the village was renamed Corby Glen in the 1950s to avoid confusion with Corby in Northamptonshire.

10. Brooke, Egleton & Gunthorpe

The rolling hills between Oakham, Rutland Water and Uppingham make for a superb walk.

THE ROUTE

I like to start and finish this one in impossibly charming Brooke, but there is very limited parking. However you can park on the verges either side of the road to the south of the village. Take the road which runs downhill to the left of the idyllic church and follow it round the left hand bend and then north out of the village past Bridge Farm. This stretch forms part of the Macmillan Way and the Rutland Round and you will soon be on a steady climb past Hillside Cottage on the left and then through two large pastures. Shortly after you pass under the overhead cables you will come to a gateway and a footpath junction. Turn right here and begin your descent towards Rutland Water, passing Brooke Covert East on the left. There are some lovely views of Oakham and beyond from this path. Keep heading gradually downhill until you cross the railway and then cross straight over the A6003 and walk down Hambleton Road into Egleton, another jewel in the Rutland crown of glorious villages.

As you arrive in Egleton you will see a footpath on the right, but for this walk it's much better to ignore this one and head to the car park for the bird watching centre. From here you can turn right on to the Rutland Water cycling and walking circuit. Follow the easy trail as it twists and turns for approximately a mile until you come to an obvious new steel kissing gate in the woods on the right with a post marker. Go through this gate and keep the hedge on your immediate right until you come back to the A6003. Cross the road and then the railway beyond and take the path gradually uphill to majestic old Gunthorpe. Keep following the posts and go past the colourful blue houses on your right and then pick up the farm track which leads west all the way back to Brooke with great views to the south.

ESSENTIAL INFORMATION

Difficulty rating

Three paws. A couple of decent climbs.

Where to park
On the verges to the south of Brooke.

Distance
Five and a half miles.

Highlights
Brooke, Egleton and Gunthorpe are all charming in their own right and there are plenty of panoramic views of Rutland from the high points.

The pooch perspective
There are sheep in some fields on the way round and you have to be careful on the Rutland Water path. And apart from the Gwash at Brooke there isn't much accessible fresh water. So be prepared in high summer.

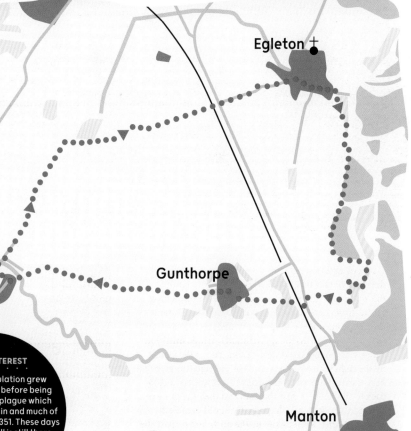

POINT OF INTEREST

Gunthorpe's population grew to several hundred before being devastated by the plague which ravaged Great Britain and much of Europe from 1347 to 1351. These days the magnificent hall is still there with its south facing aspect and there are a number of other properties on site.

11. Helpston

A serious leg stretch in poetic footsteps with plenty of ancient woodland.

THE ROUTE

You can park on Woodgate, right outside John Clare cottage where the famous peasant poet was born in 1793 and the footpath strikes out east directly opposite the Blue Bell pub. After about 200 yards turn right just after the little footbridge and after another 200 yards turn left. Follow the footpath posts and you will soon see the path cutting diagonally across a field towards College Cottages. Go through the gap in the trees and turn right to walk south through the farmyard on the farm track.

When you get to the T-junction about 300 yards south of the last farm buildings turn left on to the well-maintained road. This is Maxham's Green Road, which soon comes to the junction with Woodcroft Road where you turn right. Walk south on the road for a kilometre until you reach a right angle bend to the left at Pellett Hall.

Here you turn right onto the bridleway which ultimately leads to Woodcroft Lodge.

After a short distance on the bridleway, and just after the striking dead tree, turn left and follow the path south and around Hayes Wood. Keep going until you come to the clearly marked right turn across a picturesque field boundary towards Simon's Wood. From here keep the woods tightly to your left as you keep going back towards Helpston for a kilometre and eventually you will come to a farm track. Turn left on to the farm track and you quickly come to Heath Road.

Turn left here and then you can walk back to Broadwheel Road in Helpston down the middle of Rice Wood. Take the right turn at the end of the wood and from here it's a very short walk back to the car.

ESSENTIAL INFORMATION

Difficulty rating

Three paws. It's a long way but easy underfoot and very few obstacles.

Where to park
On Woodgate near Clare Cottage.

Distance
Five and a quarter miles.

Highlights
Surprisingly undulating around Woodcroft Lodge with plenty of picturesque woodland. A really good walk almost completely uninterrupted by stiles.

The pooch perspective
No livestock in sight when I did this walk but not much fresh water either.

Helpston

S/F

PH

POINT OF INTEREST

The thatched cottage where John Clare was born was bought by the John Clare Trust in 2005 and is now a museum. This remarkable man was born to illiterate farm-labouring parents and went to school in Glinton until the age of 12 where his lyrical talent was first nurtured. Since his death his fame has spread and he is admired far more now than he ever was in life: clarecottage.org

12. Laxton Hall and Blatherwycke

A grand old country hall, an ancient abbey, a Midsomer Murders style village and some beautiful woodland make this a welcome walk.

THE ROUTE

I parked on the road by the footpath to the church on the southern edge of Laxton, but you can also park near the village green. The footpath leads to the south east from opposite the church and immediately delivers panoramic views to the south and west.

Follow the path through the first smaller field and then down the hill to the bottom left hand corner of the next very large field. There were cows in here when I did the walk so take care. When you get to the corner go through on to the narrow country lane and turn left to walk along here for 300 yards until you come to the busy A43. Take care crossing the road and carry on up the lane opposite towards Blatherwycke.

Once you are over the first hill the noise of the main road dissipates. Stay on this quiet lane for about half a mile until you come to the edge of Blatherwycke. Turn left at the road junction and walk north with views of the lake to the east. After 300 yards you will see the footpath straight ahead where the road forks to King's Cliffe on the right and back to the A43 on the left. Take the footpath and leave the lane behind. You will now enter quite a well populated game area with partridges and pheasants

aplenty as well as a few sheep. So please do keep your dogs under very close control.

Keep heading north following the path through four field boundaries until you drop downhill, with ancient Fineshade Abbey ahead and Fineshade and Westhay Woods sprawling out to your right. Take care to find the correct route (you are now also joining the Jurassic Way) here by turning left and crossing the rather unsightly but extremely functional concrete bridge over the muddy stream. It's down in the dip before the mound that used to host St Mary's Augustinian Priory.

Once you have crossed the concrete bridge walk west across the field and then re-cross the A43 and head out into the fields where the path continues to run west through pasture land. You will see Laxton Lodge Gatehouses on your left to start with and then gradually the grand view of Laxton Hall will unfold. The path runs across the northern face of the Hall and then enters Wakerley Woods in the corner of the grassland.

Once you are in the woods it's 500 yards west and then turn left at an obvious junction for another 500 yards south before emerging from the trees to the sight of Laxton village a field away.

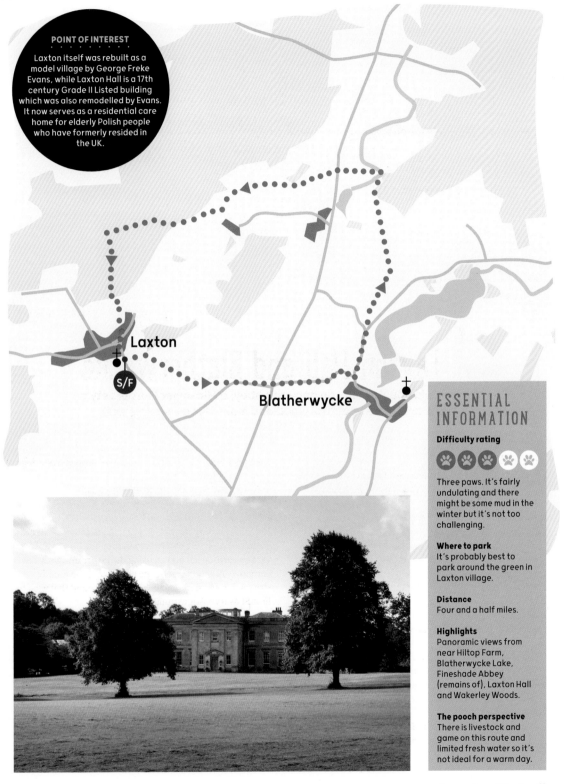

POINT OF INTEREST

Laxton itself was rebuilt as a model village by George Freke Evans, while Laxton Hall is a 17th century Grade II Listed building which was also remodelled by Evans. It now serves as a residential care home for elderly Polish people who have formerly resided in the UK.

Laxton

S/F

Blatherwycke

ESSENTIAL INFORMATION

Difficulty rating

Three paws. It's fairly undulating and there might be some mud in the winter but it's not too challenging.

Where to park
It's probably best to park around the green in Laxton village.

Distance
Four and a half miles.

Highlights
Panoramic views from near Hiltop Farm, Blatherwycke Lake, Fineshade Abbey (remains of), Laxton Hall and Wakerley Woods.

The pooch perspective
There is livestock and game on this route and limited fresh water so it's not ideal for a warm day.

13. Stamford and the Welland loop

Enjoy Stamford's honey coloured stone buildings and a decent leg stretch down by the Welland.

THE ROUTE

Park in Wharf Road car park in Stamford and head east out of town along Wharf Road, then on to St. Leonard's Street towards St Leonard's Priory at the eastern end of Priory Road. Once you have explored the ancient priory, walk east across the south of the Morrisons roundabout before taking the track down to Hudd's Mill on the right just before the new retirement home.

Follow the lane around to the left at the bottom and stay on the track to pass through the gate at the end, bringing you out into a field which is often used for sheep grazing. Carry straight on over this field and you will reach a small footbridge over the gurgling clear waters of the River Gwash. After the bridge you will quickly come to a gateway on the right just before another bridge over an old dry riverbed. Go through this gateway and follow the long winding path for the best part of a mile as it tracks the River Welland on the right. With plenty of overhanging trees there is a natural corridor which adds a little something extra to the walk.

You will eventually come to a gate to the north of the impressive stone bridge over the Welland just below Copthill School. Look out for oncoming traffic and cross over the bridge before taking a right turn through a gate in the hedge in 50 yards.

From here follow the footpath signs west (ignoring the one that branches off to the left) until you get on to another raised walkway running through the trees on the south side of the Welland, with the railway on your left. Occasional glimpses of Burghley House to the south punctuate the route as you take this peaceful path back towards town. When you reach the end of the path turn left and cross the railway. Follow the farm track up to Barnack Road and turn right to walk towards Stamford. When you get into the residential area look out for the right turn on to Water Street.

Keep walking along Water Street, past the Albert Bridge (also known as Paradise Bridge), and you will soon come to the George of Stamford with picturesque alms houses opposite. Turn right here and cross the stone bridge to head up St Mary's Hill past the town hall. Turn right at the top when you get to the King West office and walk along St Mary's Street past the magnificent Georgian Arts Centre and then through St George's Square. This is period drama heaven and you don't have to work too hard to take the imaginary step back 200 years into the peak of the Jane Austen era. From the square you can head left up St George's Street to explore even more of lovely old Stamford, or just head right down Blackfriars to Wharf Road car park.

ESSENTIAL INFORMATION

Difficulty rating

Two paws. There is nothing challenging about this walk but it can be a bit uneven underfoot in places along the paths either side of the river.

Where to park
Wharf Road car park in Stamford.

Distance
Five and a half miles.

Highlights
The honey coloured limestone used in much of the old centre of Stamford, St Leonard's Priory, the bridge at Copthill and the peaceful routes either side of the Welland.

The pooch perspective
There may be cattle or sheep in one or two fields near the river, and obviously it's a bit restricted in town but the dog will thank you in the long run for the countryside elements.

POINT OF INTEREST

For a time in the late 18th and early 19th centuries the George became famous with no fewer than 40 coaches, 'twenty up and twenty down', passing through Stamford every day. In earlier days the whole journey from London to York by stage took four days, the fare being 25 shillings inside and 18 shillings outside. In the heyday of the coaching age the time allowed for the mail coach from London to Stamford was nine hours and twenty minutes, including changes.

Uffington

Stamford

Wothorpe

Pilsgate

14. Tugby and Rolleston

Two impressive old halls bookend this wonderful walk in rolling countryside.

THE ROUTE

Tugby is on the A47 between Uppingham and Leicester and when you turn in to the village you can park anywhere, but I found my way to the Tugby Centre car park which is right at the start of the walk. This lottery-funded building is a recreation centre for the village and the large empty car park served my needs well. Turn left out of the car park and you are almost immediately out into the countryside with the A47 already a distant memory.

After the first gate turn left and cross a couple of field boundaries with views towards grand old Keythorpe Hall on your left before you reach Lake House Farm. Take the footpath off to the right just before the main farm and walk across the pasture until you reach Palmers Lane. Turn right here and walk downhill along this very peaceful country road until you reach the bridleway sign on the right near the bottom of the hill. This narrow bridleway then heads uphill steeply and,

as with all narrow bridleways in winter, it can be quite muddy but it's not impassable.

When you reach the top of the hill enjoy the great views to the north before heading down the steep bank and into the woodland around the stream in the valley bottom. It's a pretty spot and, once you are over the little footbridge and out of the wood, cross a couple of arable fields. You will soon get the sense of being in old parkland with planned plantations old and new and grass pastures. Stay on the path as it meanders down into the grounds of Rolleston Hall and just after the lake on your left the path turns right back to Tugby (it's probably worth a quick detour to the hall).

Once you are back on the eastward path to Tugby it's a pretty straight line passing Crow Wood initially on your right and then a series of fields with a stream halfway for the dog if needed. And before you know it you will be back in Tugby at the end of one of the better walks to be had in the area.

ESSENTIAL INFORMATION

Difficulty rating

Three paws. There aren't too many stiles and while it can be muddy it is pretty good going underfoot for the most part.

Where to park
Tugby Centre in the village is a lottery funded recreation facility with a large and empty car park.

Distance
Four and a half miles.

Highlights
Rolleston Hall and grounds will take you back to a forgotten way of life. Palmers Lane is a peaceful country road and the whole circuit provides variation and interest.

The pooch perspective
The route crosses two good streams for cooling off and drinking and I didn't see any livestock on my way round.

Tugby

S/F

Rolleston

Noseley

Goadby

POINT OF INTEREST

Lord Churchill, Winston Churchill's cousin, who was Lord in Waiting to Queen Victoria, bought the Rolleston estate in 1896. He built several cottages and most of the present estate buildings. In 1902 he was created Viscount Churchill of Rolleston but he subsequently sold the estate and the present hall is a much smaller version of the original.

SIX MILES PLUS

15. Belton-in-Rutland

This walk has some of Rutland's best views and will be an excellent way to burn off some of life's excesses.

THE ROUTE

Park near College Farm Lane and take this peaceful road north out of the village. It only leads to three farms so there is hardly any traffic. As the road turns to the west near its end the bridleway branches off to the right. If it's been raining recently it will be quite muddy on this stretch as the path continues up the hill so it's a good way to get warm and get the blood pumping. When you reach the top of the hill you can get your breath back whilst enjoying the glorious views of the sweeping countryside to the south. Rutland is a beautiful county, but there are not too many better views than this.

Once you have recovered from the ascent start out on the long easy stroll east along the ridgeway to Ridlington, enjoying fine views on either side, and easy conditions underfoot. You will pass two footpaths heading south down to Belton if you want to take a shortcut.

But for the full effect of this appetite-inducing walk keep going into Ridlington, passing through Wills

Farm along the way. Stay on the road as it takes one 90-degree turn to the right and then the bridleway is obvious, straight ahead as the road turns left. Head down the bridleway and take the right turn which comes up immediately. The walk changes character from here as you head downhill and briefly into the woods. The path crosses a handy stream for the dog to have a swim and a drink then heads uphill out of the woods. At the junction at the top of the hill take the path heading off at 2 o'clock. The views are still impressive from here but rather than looking down you will be looking up to strategically placed Park Farm and the hills surrounding it.

Once Park Farm is behind you there is one more climb before Belton hoves into rather spectacular view again and provides the necessary visual stimulus to finish the walk in style. And it really is a satisfying finish, as the path heads downhill, through a hedgerow and across another stream over a brand new wooden bridge, before heading into the village via a pretty little paddock.

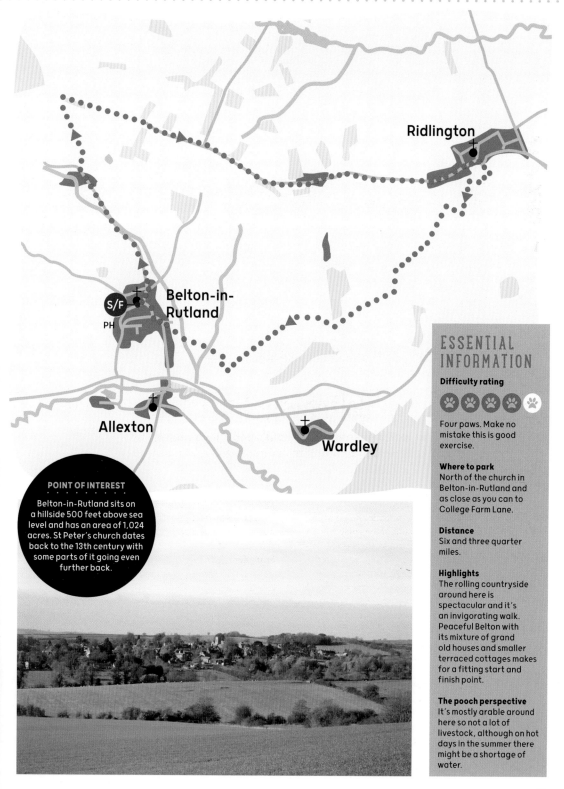

Ridlington

Belton-in-Rutland

S/F

PH

Allexton

Wardley

POINT OF INTEREST

Belton-in-Rutland sits on a hillside 500 feet above sea level and has an area of 1,024 acres. St Peter's church dates back to the 13th century with some parts of it going even further back.

ESSENTIAL INFORMATION

Difficulty rating

Four paws. Make no mistake this is good exercise.

Where to park
North of the church in Belton-in-Rutland and as close as you can to College Farm Lane.

Distance
Six and three quarter miles.

Highlights
The rolling countryside around here is spectacular and it's an invigorating walk. Peaceful Belton with its mixture of grand old houses and smaller terraced cottages makes for a fitting start and finish point.

The pooch perspective
It's mostly arable around here so not a lot of livestock, although on hot days in the summer there might be a shortage of water.

16. Braunston -in-Rutland

This west Rutland ramble takes in one of the finest villages in the area and plenty of contours.

THE ROUTE

From the church in Braunston-in-Rutland head north straight up Church Street and turn left on to High Street. After less than 100 metres take the bridleway on the right which looks like a farm track. From here it's a long uphill walk for one kilometre on the track between two hedgerows. Eventually you will come out into a grazing field where you turn left and walk across the field for 300 metres to reach a T-junction with another bridleway. The views from up here are spectacular and make the uphill start worth every step.

At the T-junction turn left on to another bridleway and keep heading downhill through the woods for a kilometre. It's charming and peaceful on this track in the summer, but avoid it in the winter when the combination of rain and horse's hooves makes it one of the muddiest routes in the area.

When you reach Braunston Road at the bottom cross straight over and go through the gates and down the tree-lined avenue to the bridge over the Gwash. After the bridge head straight up the hill to find the next footpath post and gateway and keep following the posts through a series of rolling fields. This is a surprisingly remote area and you do cross into Leicestershire briefly on this section.

Keep following the signs and you will gradually head in a south-westerly arc (ignoring any right hand turn footpaths) past Preston Lodge to the west, and down to meet the road by the Launde Abbey junction. On the day we did this walk the gate just before the road was locked, and it wasn't the easiest to clamber over with two labradors. It's rare to find a section of footpath locked like this.

When you do reach the road walk south downhill to Launde Abbey for approximately one kilometre and then turn left at the bridleway sign through Cottage Farm. Before the last large barn, make sure you bear left at the signpost and then it's a steep climb. At the top keep heading east across a couple of fields before skirting the north of Top Windmill wood. At this point stay on the bridleway and don't be distracted by a footpath to the left. Then look out for the turn to the left indicated by a wooden post with Hebes Wood written vertically on it. Take this turn and follow the route to Wood Lane and downhill back to Braunston.

ESSENTIAL INFORMATION

Difficulty rating

Five paws. A long uphill climb to start and plenty of undulations after that, and then a steep climb from Cottage Farm.

Where to park
Wherever you can in Braunston near the church and the Blue Ball.

Distance
Six miles.

Highlights
Braunston is one of the finest villages in Rutland and the Blue Ball is an excellent pub. The views from the high point and the rolling fields to the west make for great walking.

The pooch perspective
It's a good walk for the dogs but you are likely to encounter cattle and sheep along the way. The Gwash crossing comes in handy for cooling off.

POINT OF INTEREST

At the west end of the church in Braunston there is a sculpted stone, which was found when the church doorstep needed to be replaced. The slab was lifted and the carving was revealed on the underside. It was not originally a gargoyle as it has no drainage channel so its original purpose is not clear.

PH
Knossington

PH
Braunston-in-Rutland
S/F

17. Castle Bytham and Clipsham

A beautiful walk with quintessential English countryside, quarries, woodland, perfect pubs and a prison.

THE ROUTE

Park in Castle Bytham and take the footpath immediately to the right of the Castle Inn as you look at it from the road. Follow the path around the church and then the graveyard beyond and you will soon come to a field edge with a footpath sign with two options. Follow the left hand branch over the field and cross straight over Clipsham Road within five minutes.

Keep going south across another three fields (the path isn't always clear in the third field but it is there) and you will then come to a sometimes well concealed gap in the hedge leading to the narrow path between the quarries which are so characteristic of this corner of north east Rutland. This path is also the boundary between Lincolnshire and Rutland and it soon starts to head downhill. When you get to the first house on the left look out for the obvious right turn on to the farm track through the small piece of woodland. Once you are on this track follow it west for one mile, passing to the north of New Quarry House, and you will come into beautiful little Clipsham.

Walk straight ahead into the village on Main Road and turn right on to New Road before you get to the Olive Branch. Then turn right again on to West Street which

becomes Bradley Lane after the church entrance. Look out for the footpath sign on the left as you walk north along Bradley Lane and take this route out of Clipsham. From here follow the footpath signs over the peaceful fields for about a kilometre before entering Addah Wood. Very soon you will see the security fencing around the south side of HMP Stocken and this is when the woodland path turns right.

Follow the wonderful woodland path as it meanders from Addah Wood into Lady Wood before emerging into the open air on the western edge of Little Haw Wood. Keep heading north until you clear the wood and then turn right along the banks of the often dry stream. Here you leave Rutland behind for the rest of the walk.

You will now find yourself in a peaceful shallow valley with about a mile and a half to go. Just follow the stream and the signs for the first three fields and then the path breaks away from the waterway to head north east diagonally across a field towards the dismantled railway. Go under the railway in the pedestrian tunnel, which feels like the gateway to a different land, turn right and you will soon be on the main road into Castle Bytham. It's worth a stroll down Water Lane to the duck pond before retreating to the Castle Inn for some refreshments.

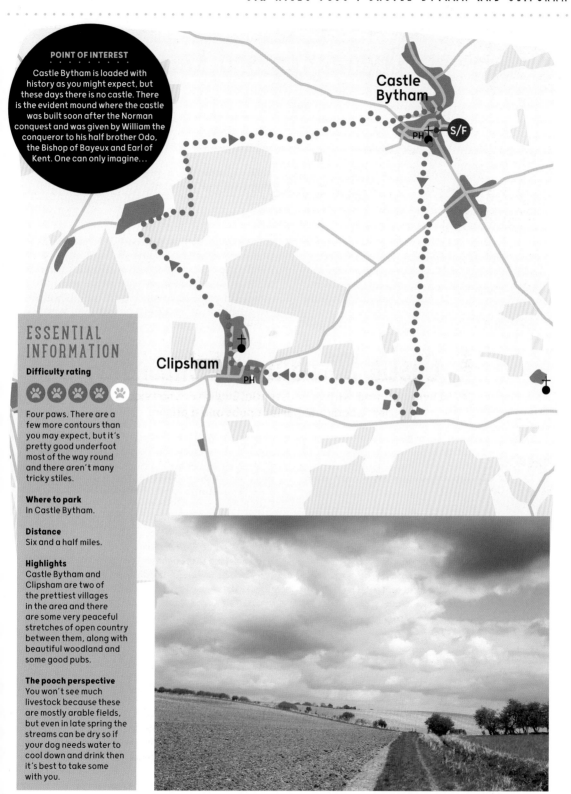

POINT OF INTEREST

Castle Bytham is loaded with history as you might expect, but these days there is no castle. There is the evident mound where the castle was built soon after the Norman conquest and was given by William the conqueror to his half brother Odo, the Bishop of Bayeux and Earl of Kent. One can only imagine…

Castle Bytham

S/F

PH

Clipsham

PH

ESSENTIAL INFORMATION

Difficulty rating

Four paws. There are a few more contours than you may expect, but it's pretty good underfoot most of the way round and there aren't many tricky stiles.

Where to park
In Castle Bytham.

Distance
Six and a half miles.

Highlights
Castle Bytham and Clipsham are two of the prettiest villages in the area and there are some very peaceful stretches of open country between them, along with beautiful woodland and some good pubs.

The pooch perspective
You won't see much livestock because these are mostly arable fields, but even in late spring the streams can be dry so if your dog needs water to cool down and drink then it's best to take some with you.

18. Duddington and Ketton

This Welland valley amble from Duddington to Ketton and back offers rural bliss and two stunning villages.

THE ROUTE

Park in Duddington and walk along Mill Street from the main junction in the middle of the village where an imposing horse chestnut stands guard over its settlement. Go downhill past the church and you will soon come to the mill on your left and the bridge over the Welland, which also marks the county boundary of Northamptonshire and Rutland. Cross the bridge and take the footpath off to the right immediately afterwards. Follow the path over another fence, under the A47 and through another gate into the large grazing field with the Welland forming one boundary.

It's a timeless rural scene and the path soon joins the tree line near the far corner and stays in the trees for 100 yards or so, before the left turn into another grazing field and up to the road to Tixover Grange.

Turn right on to the road and follow it around the sharp left turn. You can take the footpath on the right direct to Geeston and Ketton, but I would recommend staying on the road. By doing this you can create a loop to Ketton and back rather than having to retrace your steps.

So stay on the road up the hill with the disused quarry on the right, follow the road around to the right and enjoy the fine views across the Chater and Welland valleys on either side. You will also notice the newly established Rutland Vineyard which is well worth a visit. The road drops down into Geeston which is in effect a southern suburb of Ketton. Because it's such a quiet country lane there are none of the usual annoyances associated with walking along roads. You will come in on Barrowden Road which is unusually wide with houses so spread out you will think you have walked into Kentucky not Ketton.

Halfway along this residential road there is a footpath on the left, which is the western foot route across the railway and the Chater into the picturesque centre of old Ketton. It's also a good opportunity for the dog to cool off in the river and have a drink. Follow the path and you will come out by the Railway pub. From here walk down the hill to the pedestrian and vehicle bridges back over the Chater and take the footpath up to Geeston which you will see ahead as soon as you cross the footbridge. This path winds through the residential areas of Geeston, crosses the railway and ultimately joins Geeston Road. Turn right here and keep going straight until you see the path signposted to Tixover Grange to the right, as the road turns left towards Collyweston. From here the path traverses the Welland Valley for a mile and a half to Tixover Grange and here you rejoin the route back to Duddington.

ESSENTIAL INFORMATION

Difficulty rating

Three paws. It's generally pretty good underfoot but it is more than six miles.

Where to park
In Duddington.

Distance
Six and a quarter miles.

Highlights
Duddington and Ketton both have impressive village centres away from the main roads. Tranquil views of the Welland and Chater Valley.

The pooch perspective
The Chater and the Welland both offer opportunities for cooling off and a drink but there are a lot of sheep in places.

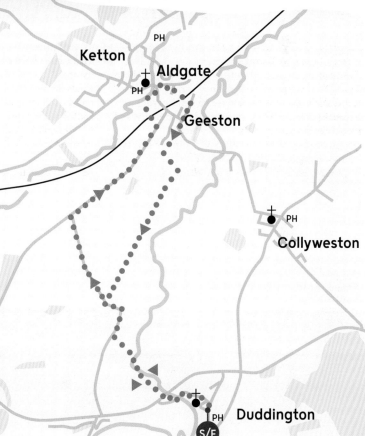

POINT OF INTEREST

Before the A43 and A47 both by-passed the village the High Street and Stamford Road in Duddington were very busy thoroughfares, but these days the village centre is surprisingly tranquil, considering its proximity to both of these main roads.

19. Stamford, Tolethorpe, Ryhall and Belmesthorpe

A pleasing blend of town and country offers some great views and plenty of pubs.

THE ROUTE

It may seem odd to start a country walk in the middle of town but I think doing it this way delivers some pleasing contrasts. So start at the Recreation Ground in Stamford where the well cared for gardens and bandstand make for a good beginning. At the road junction on the north east corner of the Recreation Ground head north up Kings Road until you get to the Welland Academy on the edge of town. Bear left here on to Churchill Road and after 200 metres take the footpath off to the right and out into the fields.

Stay on this path for the next mile and a half as it heads north past Northfields Farm. You will ultimately come to the road just near Tolethorpe. Turn left here and walk downhill for 100 metres taking care on this tricky stretch of road. Turn right and walk past the entrance to Tolethorpe Hall and you will soon come to a metal gate in the fence on the right. Go through here and over the stile in about 50 metres. Turn left and then almost immediately right to pick up the straight path downhill towards Ryhall. You will join the Gwash on your left at the bottom of this field and then follow the track up to the main road at Ryhall.

Cross the main road and turn left before turning right on to New Road into Ryhall village centre. Turn left at the Green Dragon pub and cross the bridge before turning right to walk to Belmesthorpe on the quiet lane between the two villages. Turn right at the crossroads in Belmesthorpe and then left up Castle Rise. You will see the footpath between two houses as it heads south out of the village and up the hill. Along this stretch you will be treated to the unusual sight of llamas grazing in the fields before the path crosses a grazing field and then joins a narrow bridleway between two rows of hawthorn, sloe and blackberry bushes. Turn right here and the bridleway soon comes out on to the road which leads down to Newstead. Walk along the road for about 100 metres and then take the footpath off to the right.

From here you will experience some of the best and most unexpected views of Stamford and Burghley House in the distance. The high vantage point gives a great perspective and, while Ryhall Road's industrial estates may not sound too attractive, the contrast with the church spires behind them is strangely pleasing. The path heads diagonally down to a bridge back over the Gwash and bears left across the meadow leading to an uphill track on to Ryhall Road next to the large new Alltech building.

You will quickly move from glorious countryside with stunning views into a busy retail and industrial area. Turn left and take Ryhall Road back into town past Homebase and the hospital and on to St Paul's Street where all of Stamford's marvellous shops, pubs, cafés and restaurants will cater for your every need.

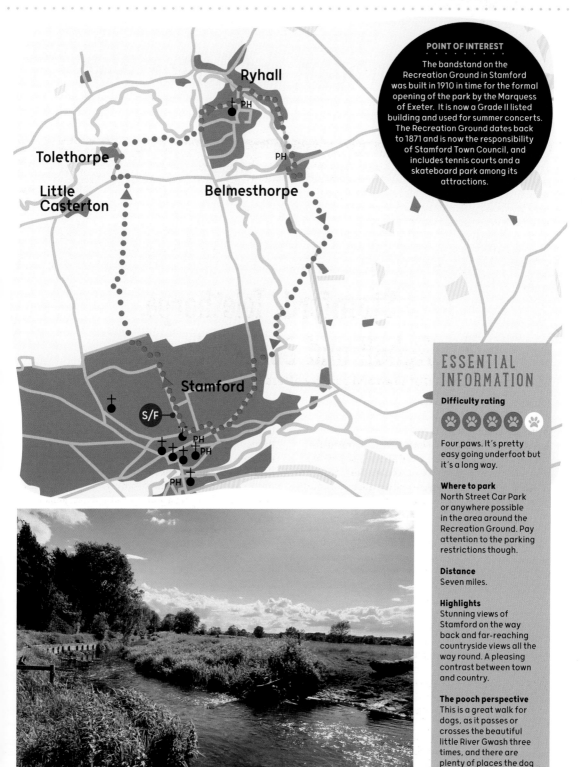

Ryhall

PH

Tolethorpe

Little
Casterton

Belmesthorpe

PH

PH

Stamford

S/F

PH
PH

PH

POINT OF INTEREST
The bandstand on the Recreation Ground in Stamford was built in 1910 in time for the formal opening of the park by the Marquess of Exeter. It is now a Grade II listed building and used for summer concerts. The Recreation Ground dates back to 1871 and is now the responsibility of Stamford Town Council, and includes tennis courts and a skateboard park among its attractions.

ESSENTIAL INFORMATION

Difficulty rating

🐾 🐾 🐾 🐾 🐾

Four paws. It's pretty easy going underfoot but it's a long way.

Where to park
North Street Car Park or anywhere possible in the area around the Recreation Ground. Pay attention to the parking restrictions though.

Distance
Seven miles.

Highlights
Stunning views of Stamford on the way back and far-reaching countryside views all the way round. A pleasing contrast between town and country.

The pooch perspective
This is a great walk for dogs, as it passes or crosses the beautiful little River Gwash three times, and there are plenty of places the dog can run free.

20. Warmington and Ashton Wold

A private woodland estate, a medieval village, some of the longest views in the area and an American war memorial make this a very worthwhile wander.

THE ROUTE

Park somewhere out of the way along Church Street in Warmington and opposite the church you will see the Nene Way heading down Long Lane. Take this path and at the bottom turn right and immediately left to find the path over a sweeping grassy ridge and furrow meadow. The path crosses the field diagonally and carries on through a thin belt of trees and hedges until it hits the hedge at the edge of the field. Here you will find a wooden bridge over the ditch followed by a path diagonally across the next field to another wooden bridge. Cross over and turn left to head uphill around the woodland edge. Take the 90-degree right turn and keep going uphill until you get to the top edge of the woodland. From here you will have extensive views of Oundle to the west and Warmington, Fotheringhay and beyond to the north.

Go through the gap in the hedge on the left and keep heading south east across the field towards Tansor Wold Farm where you turn left on to the road. Stay on the tarmac for about half a mile until you come to a road junction where you turn right off the road and into the Ashton Wold estate. From here the path heads south for a mile through the pleasant woodland which inevitably will be muddy in the winter months. Eventually you will come out on the road just by the fairytale Lutton Road Cottages.

Turn left and prepare for some time on the tarmac as you pass the entrance to Polebrook Airfield. When you get to the crossroads turn right to head to the American war memorial, which is a lot closer than the sign suggests.

To carry on your walk take the lane leading east from almost opposite the memorial and you will come into Lutton via Manor Farm. Turn left at the church and look out for the footpath sign on the right to take you through Grange Farm. There are meticulous instructions for navigating the farm on the gate but it's pretty simple if you have an OS map. Before long you will be striding out over the fields north west towards Papley Farm and the site of the medieval village of Papley with the remains of a moat still just about discernible. Go past Papley Cottages which are holiday properties and after about 200 yards turn left through the gate to head north west for a straight two kilometres. I would suggest you pick a day with no icy northwesterly wind because I can tell you from experience there is no hiding place from that here.

When you reach the road turn left and then just before Rectory Farm turn right on to the footpath which drops downhill back to Warmington. The views from here are superb and it's pretty straightforward all the way back to the car from here.

ESSENTIAL INFORMATION

Difficulty rating

Five paws. It's a long way and can be muddy on the shaded paths. Just be prepared to keep walking!

Where to park
On Church Street in Warmington near the church and Long Lane.

Distance
Nine miles.

Highlights
Some of the longest views in the area to the north, the ancient Ashton Wold estate, medieval village of Papley and the American War Memorial at Polebrook.

The pooch perspective
There are a few sheep on the way round but not many and the odd stream here and there helps for the dogs.

POINT OF INTEREST

The US War Memorial is in memory of the 175 B-17 Flying Fortresses and their crews of the 351st bombardment group who were lost during 311 group combat missions flown from RAF Polebrook in the Second World War. It's a deeply poignant reminder of these men who died a very long way from home to defend our freedom.

Warmington

PH

S/F

Ashton Wold

PH

Lutton

21. Wymondham

A rural stride out from a charming village with a windmill and a café.

THE ROUTE

Wymondham is charming without doubt but it is one of those villages which seems to take a long time to get to whichever route you choose, although that gives it a sense of remoteness which is quite attractive. Once you have arrived park up somewhere near the junction of Main Street and Butt Lane and find the footpath signposted Buckminster heading north from Main Street just east of the Edmondthorpe Road junction.

Head straight up the gradual hill on the footpath towards the dismantled railway, a reminder of a time when the village perhaps did not seem quite so remote. Once beyond the old railway the footpath heads due north and at certain times of the year stretches out into the distance like the yellow brick road. The path skirts around Mount Pleasant farmhouse and, after the farm, the path continues north through a handful of fields with a jink in a field corner to potentially catch you out and one midfield gap in the hedge after that to look out for. You soon come to Coston Covert on your left and will start to see Buckminster more clearly in the distance. Keep going following the yellow posts until the path reaches the B676

on a right angle bend. This is the most northerly point of the walk and there is a bridleway here cutting back in a south easterly direction.

After an initial drop the route climbs a bit and gives some long distance views to the south. Stay on the bridleway as it crosses the road just to the south west of Sewstern. Carry on for approximately 500 metres and then take the right followed by an almost immediate left. Then at the end of the field (in about 800 metres) make sure you look out for the westward bridleway in the hedge junction.

Once you are heading west the path initially goes straight over the first field but then sticks to the boundaries for a few smaller fields and is pretty well signposted. After you pass Marriot's Spinney (the second piece of woodland) on your left take the next right to hit the road. Turn left here and stay on the road for 200 yards. Once you have taken the right hand turn on the road you will soon see the footpath on the right in a hedge. Head down here and take the left turn at the stream. This path takes you down through the grassland and then through the small wood to rejoin the path back over the railway. From there it's a short stroll back to the village.

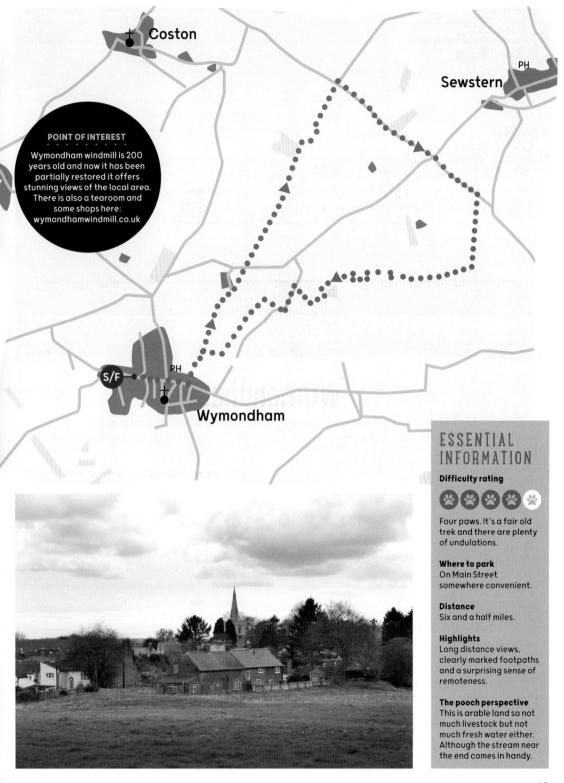

Coston

Sewstern

PH

POINT OF INTEREST

Wymondham windmill is 200 years old and now it has been partially restored it offers stunning views of the local area. There is also a tearoom and some shops here: wymondhamwindmill.co.uk

PH

S/F

Wymondham

ESSENTIAL INFORMATION

Difficulty rating

Four paws. It's a fair old trek and there are plenty of undulations.

Where to park
On Main Street somewhere convenient.

Distance
Six and a half miles.

Highlights
Long distance views, clearly marked footpaths and a surprising sense of remoteness.

The pooch perspective
This is arable land so not much livestock but not much fresh water either. Although the stream near the end comes in handy.

Great food for hungry walkers

How to find the best places to eat once you have finished your walk.

If you love food, drink, pubs and restaurants, then check out the work of our friends at the Great Food Club in rural Leicestershire. The Great Food Club is a guide to the East Midlands' best food and drink independents and operates across three platforms – website, annual printed book, and phone app.

Head over to their website (greatfoodclub.co.uk) to search the 650 plus places they recommend.

Once you've had a look, you may want to join the club and get your hands on a copy of their printed annual handbook along with a membership card that unlocks more than 120 special offers at places such as Hambleton Hall near Oakham, The Olive Branch in Clipsham and the Hammer & Pincers in Wymeswold.

Here are three Great Food Club recommendations that you might want to consider after enjoying a walk.

• Lambert's Kitchen, Stamford

A finalist in the Great Food Club Awards 2019/2020, it's a superb place for breakfast or lunch. Card-carrying GFC Members get 10 per cent off the bill.

• The Jackson Stops, Stretton

The thatched Jackson Stops is as pretty as a picture. It serves excellent food, too. Card-carrying GFC Members get 10 per cent off food from Monday to Friday.

• Sarpech, Oakham

This stylish Indian restaurant and wine bar offers excellent Indian food and top-class service. Card-carrying GFC Members get 10 per cent off.